POEMS

Feasts and Fasts

Christina Rossetti

Introduction by Robert Van de Weyer

Fount
An Imprint of HarperCollinsPublishers

Fount Paperbacks is an Imprint of
HarperCollins*Religious*
Part of HarperCollins*Publishers*
77–85 Fulham Palace Road, London W6 8JB

This edition first published in Great Britain
in 1996 by Fount Paperbacks

1 3 5 7 9 10 8 6 4 2

Copyright © in the Introduction 1996
by Robert Van de Weyer

A catalogue record for this book is
available from the British Library

ISBN 0 00 627995 3

Printed and bound in Great Britain by
Caledonian International Book Manufacturing Ltd, Glasgow, G64

POEMS

Feasts and Fasts

Contents

Introduction

Outwardly Christina's life was almost wholly uneventful. She never married, spurning two suitors on religious grounds, she had few social contacts outside her own family, and she rarely travelled. Apart from a few months as a teacher, her work was conducted entirely at home. And in so far as she was aware of her growing fame – she was even mentioned as a possible successor to Tennyson as Poet Laureate – she felt it as an awesome responsibility. Yet fame grew out of a turbulent and passionate inward life that found expression in her faith and in her verse. She brought together religious devotion and poetic genius in a way that few have equalled.

Christina Rossetti was born in London on 5 December 1830. Her father Gabriele was a poet and political agitator who in 1824 was condemned to death by the government of Naples for his liberal views. He escaped to Malta, disguised as a sailor, and then continued to England; there he earned a modest income as a teacher, becoming professor of Italian at the new University of London, and drew round himself a circle of other poets and political exiles from Italy. Christina's mother was also Italian. As a young woman she had been attracted by Gabriele's radical attitudes; but once she settled as his wife in England she became a fervent Anglican, and tried to impose the highest standards of Victorian piety and respectability on their new home.

Before she could even read and write Christina showed an extraordinary facility for composing verses; and throughout her childhood she filled notebooks with poems. By her late teens she was an accomplished poet; indeed, some of her finest work dates from this early period. The diverse influences of her father and mother were already visible: from her father she inherited a vivid and at times wild imagination, which enjoyed playing with metaphors and paradoxes, and from her mother she inherited a profound and devout faith, with a passionate attachment to the person of Christ at its centre. Occasionally she allowed her faith to stifle her imagination, expressing herself in the conventional metaphors of religion, but more often she tackled familiar spiritual themes with astonishing freshness and intensity.

In 1850 Gabriele Rossetti contracted consumption, and spent the remaining four years of his life as an invalid. His wife now took up teaching, and in 1853, with Christina's help, opened her own school. This was a financial failure, and the family was only saved from ruin when the younger of her brothers, William Michael, got a well-paid job as a tax inspector. In the meantime, her older brother, Dante Gabriel, had become one of the leaders of the Pre-Raphaelite Brotherhood, a group of young artists and writers seeking to revive medieval styles and techniques. Christina's poetry was first published in the Brotherhood's magazine. Her pale, fragile beauty appealed to the Pre-Raphaelite eye, so she became the inspiration of several of the figures in their pictures. One of the Brotherhood, James Collinson, proposed marriage; initially she accepted him, eventually breaking the engagement because she regarded her own Anglican faith as incompatible with his Catholicism. But her contact with the Brotherhood, and especially the influence of her brother, inspired her to become more adventurous in her poetic imagery, and more fervent and direct in the emotions she revealed.

In 1862 the first major volume of her poetry was published, followed by a second volume in 1866. These had a huge impact, establishing her as one of the leading poets of her day. At around this time she received a second offer of marriage, from Bagot Cayley, a distinguished scholar. She fully reciprocated his love, but in this case his agnosticism forced her to refuse. They remained friends, writing frequently to one another. When he died some years later she visited his house, and placed white flowers in his lifeless hands.

The continuing pain of this unfulfilled passion stimulated her saddest and most powerful verses.

Christina was stricken by Graves' disease in 1871, which marred her looks, confining her almost entirely to the family house in Bloomsbury. She believed that earthly suffering would be rewarded with heavenly joy; and the relationship between earth and heaven, life and death, became an increasing preoccupation. Whereas her earlier poetry had covered a wide range of subjects, her verses from this time on were almost entirely religious. The monotony of her existence was alleviated by her strict observance of the feasts and fasts that punctuate the Christian calendar; some of her finest religious verses focus on these, including her two most famous poems which have been set to music as carols, 'In the bleak mid-winter' and 'Love came down at Christmas'. Much of her religious poetry was brought together in 1893 in a single volume published by S.P.C.K. She also wrote a number of prose works on religious themes, including a long commentary on the Apocalypse.

Christina's mother died in 1886, and thereafter her own life was blighted by ill health. She suffered a chronic heart complaint, and in 1891 developed cancer. She survived major surgery, but the cancer returned, and she died on 29 December 1894. She was buried in the family grave in Highgate Cemetery. In the decades after her death her reputation as a poet diminished as her particular form of religion came to be regarded as sentimental and unduly pious; even her most ardent admirers would admit that some of her verses are syrupy, while others have a didactic tone. But more recently, as the Victorian age has swung back into secular and spiritual fashion, there is a new appreciation of her work. She was a prolific writer, so any volume of her poetry must be selective. The present book concentrates on her poems marking the feasts and fasts of the Christian year. It can be kept at the bedside, to be dipped into throughout the year; and many of the poems could be read aloud as acts of worship.

ROBERT VAN DE WEYER

POEMS

Advent

THIS ADVENT MOON

This Advent moon shines cold and
  clear,
 These Advent nights are long;
Our lamps have burned year after
   year
  And still their flame is strong.
'Watchman, what of the night?' we
   cry,
  Heart-sick with hope deferred:
'No speaking signs are in the sky,'
  Is still the watchman's word.

The Porter watches at the gate,
  The servants watch within;
The watch is long betimes and late,
  The prize is slow to win.
'Watchman, what of the night?'
   But still
  His answer sounds the same:
'No daybreak tops the utmost hill,
  Nor pale our lamps of flame.'

One to another hear them speak
   The patient virgins wise:
'Surely He is not far to seek'
   'All night we watch and rise.'
'The days are evil looking back,
   The coming days are dim;
Yet count we not His promise slack,
   But watch and wait for Him.'

One with another, soul with soul,
   They kindle fire from fire:
'Friends watch us who have touched
     the goal.'
   'They urge us, come up higher.'
'With them shall rest our waysore
     feet,
   With them is built our home,
With Christ.' – 'They sweet, but
     He most sweet,
   Sweeter than honeycomb.'

There no more parting, no more pain.
   The distant ones brought near,
The lost so long are found again,
   Long lost but longer dear:
Eye hath not seen, ear hath not
     heard,
   Nor heart conceived that rest,
With them our good things long
     deferred,
   With Jesus Christ our Best.

We weep because the night is long,
  We laugh for day shall rise,
We sing a slow contented song
  And knock at Paradise.
Weeping we hold Him fast Who
    wept
  For us, we hold Him fast;
And will not let Him go except
  He bless us first or last.

Weeping we hold Him fast tonight;
  We will not let Him go
Till daybreak smite our wearied
    sight
  And summer smite the snow:
Then figs shall bud, and dove with
    dove
  Shall coo the livelong day;
Then He shall say, 'Arise, My love,
  My fair one, come away.'

2 May 1858

THE BRIDEGROOM COMETH

Behold, the Bridegroom cometh:
    go ye out
With lighted lamps and garlands
    round about
To meet Him in a rapture with a
    shout.

It may be at the midnight, black as
    pitch,
Earth shall cast up her poor, cast
    up her rich.

It may be at the crowing of the
    cock
Earth shall upheave her depth,
    uproot her rock.

For lo, the Bridegroom fetcheth
    home the Bride:
His Hands are Hands she knows,
    she knows His Side.

Like pure Rebekah at the appointed
    place,
Veiled, she unveils her face to meet
    His Face.

Like great Queen Esther in her
    triumphing,
She triumphs in the Presence of her
    King.

His Eyes are as a Dove's, and she's
    Dove-eyed;
He knows His lovely mirror, sister,
    Bride.

He speaks with Dove-voice of
    exceeding love,
And she with love-voice of an
    answering Dove.

Behold, the Bridegroom cometh:
    go we out
With lamps ablaze and garlands
    round about
To meet Him in a rapture with a
    shout.

Before 1886

EARTH GROWN OLD

Earth grown old, yet still so green,
    Deep beneath her crust of
      cold
Nurses fire unfelt, unseen:
    Earth grown old.

    We who live are quickly
      told:
Millions more lie hid between
    Inner swathings of her fold.

When will fire break up her screen?
    When will life burst thro' her
      mould?
Earth, earth, earth, thy cold is keen,
    Earth grown old.

Before 1886

Christmas

CHRISTMAS HATH A DARKNESS

Christmas hath a darkness
  Brighter than the blazing noon,
Christmas hath a chillness
  Warmer than the heat of June,
Christmas hath a beauty
  Lovelier than the world can show:
For Christmas bringeth Jesus,
  Brought for us so low.

Earth, strike up your music,
  Birds that sing and bells that ring;
Heaven hath answering music
  For all Angels soon to sing:
Earth, put on your whitest
  Bridal robe of spotless snow:
For Christmas bringeth Jesus,
  Brought for us so low.

Before 1886

A CAROL FOR CHILDREN

The Shepherds had an Angel,
  The Wise Men had a star,
But what have I, a little child,
  To guide me home from far,
  Where glad stars sing together
  And singing angels are? –

Lord Jesus is my Guardian,
  So I can nothing lack:
The lambs lie in His bosom
  Along life's dangerous track:
The wilful lambs that go astray
  He bleeding fetches back.

Lord Jesus is my guiding star,
  My beacon-light in heaven:
He leads me step by step along
  The path of life uneven:
He, true light, leads me to that
    land
  Whose day shall be as seven.

Those Shepherds through the lonely
    night
  Sat watching by their sheep,
Until they saw the heavenly host
  Who neither tire nor sleep,
  All singing 'Glory glory'
  In festival they keep.

Christ watches me, His little lamb,
    Cares for me day and night,
That I may be His own in heaven:
    So angels clad in white
    Shall sing their 'Glory glory'
    For my sake in the height.

    The Wise Men left their country
    To journey morn by morn,
With gold and frankincense and
       myrrh,
    Because the Lord was born:
    God sent a star to guide them
    And sent a dream to warn.

    My life is like their journey,
      Their star is like God's book;
I must be like those good Wise Men
    With heavenward heart and
       look:
But shall I give no gifts to God? –
    What precious gifts they took!

Lord, I will give my love to Thee,
    Than gold much costlier,
Sweeter to Thee than frankincense,
    More prized than choicest
       myrrh:
Lord, make me dearer day by day,
    Day by day holier;

Nearer and dearer day by day:
    Till I my voice unite,
  And sing my 'Glory glory'
    With angels clad in white;
All 'Glory glory' given to Thee
    Through all the heavenly height.

1856

A CHIMING FOR CHRISTMAS

Whoso hears a chiming for
    Christmas at the nighest
  Hears a sound like Angels-
    chanting in their glee,
Hears a sound like palm boughs
    waving in the highest,
  Hears a sound like ripple of a
    crystal sea.

Sweeter than a prayer-bell for a
    saint in dying,
  Sweeter than a death-bell for a
    saint at rest,
Music struck in Heaven with earth's
    faint replying,
  'Life is good, and death is good,
    for Christ is Best.'

circa 1887

IN THE BLEAK MID-WINTER

In the bleak mid-winter
  Frosty wind made moan,
Earth stood hard as iron,
  Water like a stone;
Snow had fallen, snow on snow,
  Snow on snow,
In the bleak mid-winter
  Long ago.

Our God, Heaven cannot hold
  Him
  Nor earth sustain;
Heaven and earth shall flee away
  When He comes to reign:
In the bleak mid-winter
  A stable-place sufficed
The Lord God Almighty
  Jesus Christ.

Enough for Him, whom cherubim
  Worship night and day,
A breastful of milk
  And a mangerful of hay;
Enough for Him, whom angels
  Fall down before,
The ox and ass and camel
  Which adore.

Angels and archangels
  May have gathered there,
Cherubim and seraphim
  Thronged the air;
But only His mother
  In her maiden bliss
Worshipped the Beloved
  With a kiss.

What can I give Him,
  Poor as I am?
If I were a shepherd
  I would bring a lamb,
If I were a Wise Man
  I would do my part, –
Yet what I can I give Him,
  Give my heart.

Before 1872

A BABY IS A HARMLESS THING

A baby is a harmless thing
  And wins our hearts with one
    accord,
And Flower of Babies was their
    King,
  Jesus Christ our Lord:
Lily of lilies He
Upon His Mother's knee;
Rose of roses, soon to be
Crowned with thorns on leafless
    tree.

A lamb is innocent and mild
  And merry on the soft green sod;
And Jesus Christ, the Undefiled,
  Is the Lamb of God:
Only spotless He
Upon His Mother's knee;
White and ruddy, soon to be
Sacrificed for you and me.

Nay, lamb is not so sweet a word,
  Nor lily half so pure a name;
Another name our hearts hath stirred,
  Kindling them to flame:
'Jesus' certainly
Is music and melody:
Heart with heart in harmony
Carol we and worship we.

Before 1886

LOVE CAME DOWN AT CHRISTMAS

Love came down at Christmas,
　　Love all lovely, Love Divine;
Love was born at Christmas,
　　Star and Angels gave the sign.

Worship we the Godhead,
　　Love Incarnate, Love Divine;
Worship we our Jesus:
　　But wherewith for sacred sign?

Love shall be our token,
　　Love be yours and love be mine,
Love to God and all men,
　　Love for plea and gift and sign.

Before 1886

Holy Innocents

THEY SCARCELY WAKED

They scarcely waked before they
    slept,
  They scarcely wept before they
    laughed;
  They drank indeed death's bitter
    draught,
But all its bitterest dregs were
    kept
And drained by Mothers while they
    wept.

From Heaven the speechless Infants
    speak:
  Weep not (they say), our Mothers
    dear,
  For swords nor sorrows come
    not here.
Now we are strong who were so
    weak,
And all is ours we could not seek.

We bloom among the blooming
   flowers,
  We sing among the singing
    birds;
  Wisdom we have who wanted
    words:
Here morning knows not evening
    hours,
All's rainbow here without the
    showers.

And softer than our Mother's breast,
  And closer than our Mother's
    arm,
  Is here the Love that keeps us
    warm
And broods above our happy nest.
Dear Mothers, come: for Heaven
    is best.

Before 1882

UNSPOTTED LAMBS

Unspotted lambs to follow the
    one Lamb,
  Unspotted doves to wait on the
    one Dove;
To whom Love saith, 'Be with Me
    where I am,'
And lo their answer unto Love is
    love.

For tho' I know not any note they
    know,
  Nor know one word of all their
    song above,
I know Love speaks to them, and
    even so
  I know the answer unto Love is
    love.

Before 1893

Epiphany

THY LOVELY SAINTS

Thy lovely saints do bring Thee love,
  Incense and joy and gold;
Fair star with star, fair dove with
    dove,
  Beloved by Thee of old.
I, Master, neither star nor dove,
  Have brought Thee sins and
    tears;
Yet I too bring a little love
  Amid my flaws and fears.
A trembling love that faints and
    fails
  Yet still is love of Thee,
A wondering love that hopes and
    hails
  Thy boundless Love of me;
Love kindling faith and pure desire,
  Love following on to bliss,
A spark, O Jesu, from Thy fire,
  A drop from Thine abyss.

Before 1893

LORD BABE

'Lord Babe, if Thou art He
  We sought for patiently,
Where is Thy court?
Hither may prophecy and star
    resort;
Men heed not their report.' –
  'Bow down and worship, righteous
    man:
  This Infant of a span
  Is He man sought for since the
    world began!' –
'Then, Lord, accept my gold, too
    base a thing
For Thee, of all kings King.' –

'Lord Babe, despite Thy youth
I hold Thee of a truth
Both Good and Great:
But wherefore dost Thou keep so
    mean a state,
Low-lying desolate?' –
  'Bow down and worship, righteous
    seer:
  The Lord our God is here
  Approachable, Who bids us all
    draw near.' –
'Wherefore to Thee I offer
    frankincense,
Thou Sole Omnipotence.' –

'But I have only brought
Myrrh; no wise afterthought
Instructed me
To gather pearls or gems, or choice
  to see
Coral or ivory.' –
  'Not least thine offering proves
    thee wise:
  For myrrh means sacrifice,
  And He that lives, this Same is
    He that dies.' –
'Then here is myrrh: alas, yea
    woe is me
That myrrh befitteth Thee.' –

Myrrh, frankincense, and gold:
And lo from wintry fold
Good-will doth bring
A Lamb, the innocent likeness of
    this King
Whom stars and seraphs sing:
  And lo the bird of love, a Dove,
  Flutters and coos above:
  And Dove and Lamb and Babe
    agree in love: –
Come all mankind, come all creation
    hither,
Come, worship Christ together.

Before 1886

TREMBLING BEFORE THEE

Trembling before Thee we fall
　　down to adore Thee,
　Shamefaced and trembling we
　　lift our eyes to Thee:
O First and with the last! annul
　　our ruined past,
　Rebuild us to Thy glory, set us
　　free
　From sin and from sorrow to fall
　　down and worship Thee.

Full of pity view us, stretch Thy
　　sceptre to us,
　Bid us live that we may give
　　ourselves to Thee:
O faithful Lord and true! stand
　　up for us and do,
　Make us lovely, make us new,
　　set us free –
　Heart and soul and spirit – to
　　bring all and worship Thee.

Before 1893

Candlemas

FIRSTFRUITS

O firstfruits of our grain,
Infant and Lamb appointed to be
    slain,
A Virgin and two doves were all
    Thy train,
With one old man for state,
When Thou didst enter first Thy
    Father's gate.

Since then Thy train hath been
Freeman and bondman, bishop, king
    and queen,
With flaming candles and with
    garlands green:
Oh happy all who wait
One day or thousand days around
    Thy gate!

And these have offered Thee,
Beside their hearts, great stores for
    charity,
Gold, frankincense, and myrrh; if
    such may be
For savour or for state
Within the threshold of Thy golden
    gate.

Then snowdrops and my heart
I'll bring, to find those blacker than
    Thou art:
Yet, loving Lord, accept us in good
    part;
And give me grace to wait,
A bruisèd reed bowed low before
    Thy gate.

Before 1882

A CANDLEMAS DIALOGUE

'Love brought Me down: and
    cannot love make thee
Carol for joy to Me?
Hear cheerful robin carol from his
    tree,
Who owes not half to Me
I won for thee.'

'Yea, Lord, I hear his carol's
    wordless voice;
And well may he rejoice
Who hath not heard of death's
    discordant noise.
So might I too rejoice
With such a voice.'

'True, thou hast compassed death:
    but hast not thou
The tree of life's own bough?
Am I not Life and Resurrection
    now?
My Cross, balm-bearing bough
For such as thou.'

'Ah me, Thy Cross! – but that
    seems far away;
Thy Cradle-song today
I too would raise and worship Thee
    and pray:
Not empty, Lord, today
Send me away.'

'If thou wilt not go empty, spend
    thy store;
And I will give thee more,
Yea, make thee ten times richer than
    before.
Give more and give yet more
Out of thy store.'

'Because Thou givest me Thyself, I
    will
Thy blessed word fulfil,
Give with both hands, and hoard by
    giving still:
Thy pleasure to fulfil,
And work Thy Will.'

Before 1891

Lent

ASH WEDNESDAY – I

Jesus, do I love Thee?
Thou art far above me,
Seated out of sight,
Hid in heavenly light
Of most highest height.
Martyred hosts implore Thee,
Seraphs fall before Thee,
Angels and Archangels,
Cherub throngs adore Thee.
Blessed she that bore Thee!
All the saints approve Thee,
All the virgins love Thee.
I show as a blot
Blood hath cleansèd not,
As a barren spot
In thy fruitful lot;
I, fig-tree fruit-unbearing,
Thou, righteous Judge unsparing:
What canst Thou do more to me
That shall not more undo me?
Thy Justice hath a sound,
'Why cumbereth it the ground?'
Thy Love with stirrings stronger
Pleads, 'Give it one year longer.'

Thou giv'st me time: but who
Save Thou shall give me dew,
Shall feed my root with blood
And stir my sap for good? –
Oh by Thy gifts that shame me
Give more lest they condemn me.
Good Lord, I ask much of Thee,
But most I ask to love Thee:
Kind Lord, be mindful of me,
Love me and make me love Thee.

21 March 1859

ASH WEDNESDAY – II

My God, my God, have mercy on
   my sin,
For it is great; and if I should begin
To tell it all, the day would be too
   small
  To tell it in.

My God, Thou wilt have mercy on
   my sin
For Thy Love's sake: yea, if I should
   begin
To tell This all, the day would be
   too small
  To tell it in.

Before 1886

LAST NOT FIRST

It is good to be last not first,
    Pending the present distress;
It is good to hunger and thirst,
    So it be for righteousness.
It is good to spend and be spent,
    It is good to watch and to pray:
Life and Death make a goodly Lent
    So it leads us to Easter Day.

Before 1886

TOO LATE

Contempt and pangs and haunting
     fears –
  Too late for hope, too late for ease,
   Too late for rising from the
      dead;
  Too late, too late to bend my
      knees,
   Or bow my head,
  Or weep, or ask for tears.

Hark! … One I hear Who calls
     to me:
  'Give Me thy thorn and grief
     and scorn,
   Give Me thy ruin and regret.
  Press on thro' darkness toward
     the morn:
   One loves thee yet:
  Have I forgotten thee?'

Lord, Who art Thou? Lord, is it
     Thou
  My Lord and God Lord Jesus
     Christ?
   How said I that I sat alone
  And desolate and unsufficed?
   Surely a stone
  Would raise Thy praises now!

Before 1893

THE THREE ENEMIES

The Flesh

'Sweet, thou art pale.'
                    'More pale to see,
Christ hung upon the cruel tree
And bore His Father's wrath for me.'

'Sweet, thou art sad.'
                    'Beneath a rod
More heavy, Christ for my sake trod
The winepress of the wrath of God.'

'Sweet, thou art weary.'
                    'Not so Christ;
Whose mighty love of me sufficed
For Strength, Salvation, Eucharist.'

'Sweet, thou art footsore.'
                    'If I bleed,
His feet have bled; yea in my need
His Heart once bled for mine indeed.'

The World

'Sweet, thou art young.'
                    'So He was young
Who for my sake in silence hung
Upon the Cross with Passion wrung.'

'Look, thou art fair.'
                    'He was more fair
Than men, Who deigned for me to
    wear
A visage marred beyond compare.'

'And thou hast riches.'
                              'Daily bread:
All else is His: Who, living, dead,
For me lacked where to lay His
        Head.'

'And life is sweet.'
                              'It was not so
To Him, Whose Cup did overflow
With mine unutterable woe.'

The Devil

'Thou drinkest deep.'
                'When Christ would sup
He drained the dregs from out my
        cup:
So how should I be lifted up?'

'Thou shalt win Glory.'
                              'In the skies,
Lord Jesus, cover up mine eyes
Lest they should look on vanities.'

'Thou shalt have Knowledge.'
                        'Helpless dust!
In thee, O Lord, I put my trust:
Answer Thou for me, Wise and Just.'

'And Might.' –
                'Get thee behind me, Lord,
Who hast redeemed and not abhorred
My soul, oh keep it by Thy Word.'
1851

GOOD LORD

Good Lord, today
I scarce find breath to say:
　Scourge, but receive me.
For stripes are hard to bear, but
　　worse
Thy intolerable curse;
　So do not leave me.

Good Lord, lean down
In pity, tho' Thou frown;
　Smite, but retrieve me:
For so Thou hold me up to stand
And kiss Thy smiting hand,
　It less will grieve me.

Before 1893

Holy Week

I LIFT MINE EYES

I lift mine eyes, and see
Thee, tender Lord, in pain upon the
    tree,
Athirst for my sake and athirst for
    me.

'Yea, look upon Me there,
Compassed with thorns and bleeding
    everywhere,
For thy sake bearing all, and glad
    to bear.'

I lift my heart to pray:
Thou Who didst love me all that
    darkened day,
Wilt Thou not love me to the end
    alway?

'Yea, thee My wandering sheep,
Yea, thee My scarlet sinner slow to
    weep,
Come to Me, I will love thee and
    will keep.'

Yet am I racked with fear:
Behold the unending outer darkness
    drear,
Behold the gulf unbridgeable and
    near!

'Nay, fix thy heart, thine eyes,
Thy hope upon My boundless
    sacrifice:
Will I lose lightly one so dear–
    bought prize?'

Ah Lord, it is not Thou,
Thou that wilt fail; yet woe is me
    for how
Shall I endure who half am failing
    now?

'Nay, weld thy resolute will
To Mine: glance not aside for good
    or ill:
I love thee; trust Me still and love
    Me still.'

Yet Thou Thyself hast said,
When Thou shalt sift the living from
    the dead
Some must depart shamed and un–
    comforted.

'Judge not before that day:
Trust Me with all thy heart, even
    tho' I slay:
Trust Me in love, trust on, love on,
    and pray.'

Before 1893

ONCE I ACHED

Once I ached for thy dear sake:
Wilt thou cause Me now to ache?
Once I bled for thee in pain:
Wilt thou rend My Heart again?
Crown of thorns and shameful tree,
Bitter death I bore for thee,
Bore My Cross to carry thee,
And wilt thou have nought of Me?

1853

CHRIST'S HEART WAS WRUNG FOR ME

Christ's Heart was wrung for me,
        if mine is sore;
    And if my feet are weary, His
        have bled;
    He had no place wherein to lay
        His Head;
If I am burdened, He was burdened
    more.
The cup I drink He drank of long
        before;
    He felt the unuttered anguish
        which I dread;
    He hungered Who the hungry
        thousands fed,
And thirsted Who the world's re-
    freshment bore.
If grief be such a looking-glass as
        shows
    Christ's Face and man's in some
        sort made alike,
        Then grief is pleasure with a
        subtle taste:
        Wherefore should any fret or
        faint or haste?
Grief is not grievous to a soul that
        knows
    Christ comes, – and listens for
        that hour to strike.

Before 1886

THE HEART KNOWETH
ITS OWN BITTERNESS

Weep yet awhile, –
Weep till that day shall dawn
  when thou shalt smile:
Watch till the day
When all save only love shall pass
  away.

Weep, sick and lonely,
Bow thy heart to tears,
For none shall guess the secret
Of thy griefs and fears.
Weep, till the day dawn,
  Refreshing dew:
  Weep till the spring:
  For genial showers
  Bring up the flowers,
  And thou shalt sing
In summertime of blossoming.

Heart-sick and silent,
Weep and watch in pain.
  Weep for hope perished,
  Not to live again:
  Weep for love's hope and fear
  And passion vain.
  Watch till the day
When all save only love shall pass
  away.

Then love rejoicing
Shall forget to weep:
Shall hope or fear no more,
Or watch, or sleep,
But only love and cease not,
Deep beyond deep.
Now we sow love in tears,
But then shall reap.
Have patience as the Lord's own
flock of sheep:
Have patience with His love
Who died below, who lives for thee
above.

1852

THE GREAT VINE

The great Vine left its glory to
    reign as Forest King.
'Nay,' quoth the lofty forest trees,
    'we will not have this thing;
We will not have this supple one
    enring us with its ring.
Lo from immemorial time our might
    towers shadowing:
Not we were born to curve and
    droop, not we to climb and
    cling:
We buffet back the buffeting wind,
    tough to its buffeting:
We screen great beasts, the wild
    fowl build in our heads and
    sing,
Every bird of every feather from off
    our tops takes wing:
I a king, and thou a king, and what
    king shall be our king?'

Nevertheless the great Vine stooped
    to be the Forest King,
While the forest swayed and mur-
    mured like seas that are tem-
    pesting:
Stooped and drooped with thousand
    tendrils in thirsty languishing;
Bowed to earth and lay on earth for
    earth's replenishing;
Put off sweetness, tasted bitterness,
    endured time's fashioning;

Put off life and put on death: and
    lo it was all to bring
All its fellows down to a death
    which hath lost the sting,
All its fellows up to a life in endless
    triumphing, –
I a king, and thou a king, and this
    King to be our King.

Before 1886

IT IS FINISHED

Dear Lord, let me recount to Thee
Some of the great things Thou hast
    done
      For me, even me
      Thy little one.

It was not I that cared for Thee, –
But Thou didst set Thy heart upon
    Me, even me
    Thy little one.

And therefore was it sweet to Thee
To leave Thy Majesty and Throne,
    And grow like me
    A Little One,

A swaddled Baby on the knee
Of a dear Mother of Thine own,
    Quite weak like me
    Thy little one.

Thou didst assume my misery,
And reap the harvest I had sown,
    Comforting me
    Thy little one.

Jerusalem and Galilee, –
Thy love embraced not those alone,
    But also me
    Thy little one.

Thy unblemished Body on the
    Tree
Was bared and broken to atone
    For me, for me
    Thy little one.

Thou lovedst me upon the Tree, –
Still me, hid by the ponderous
    stone, –
    Me always – me
    Thy little one.

And love of me arose with Thee
When death fell and lay overthrown:
    Thou lovedst me
    Thy little one.

And love of me went up with Thee
To sit upon Thy Father's Throne:
    Thou lovest me
    Thy little one.

Lord, as Thou me, so would I Thee
Love in pure love's communion,
    For Thou lov'st me
    Thy little one:

Which love of me bring back with
    Thee
To Judgment when the Trump is
    blown,
    Still loving me
    Thy little one.

Before 1882

GOOD FRIDAY MORNING

'Bearing His Cross.'

Up Thy Hill of Sorrows
   Thou all alone,
Jesus, man's Redeemer,
   Climbing to a Throne:
Thro' the world triumphant,
   Thro' the Church in pain,
Which think to look upon Thee
   No more again.

Upon my hill of sorrows
   I, Lord, with Thee,
Cheered, upheld, yea carried
   If a need should be:
Cheered, upheld, yea carried,
   Never left alone,
Carried in Thy heart of hearts
   To a throne.

Before 1893

BENEATH THY CROSS

Am I a stone, and not a sheep,
　That I can stand, O Christ,
　　beneath Thy cross,
　To number drop by drop Thy
　　Blood's slow loss,
And yet not weep?

Not so those women loved
　Who with exceeding grief
　　lamented Thee;
　Not so fallen Peter weeping
　　bitterly;
Not so the thief was moved;

Not so the Sun and Moon
　Which hid their faces in a
　　starless sky,
A horror of great darkness at broad
　　noon –
　I, only I.

Yet give not o'er,
　But seek Thy sheep, true Shepherd
　　of the flock;
Greater than Moses, turn and look
　　once more
　And smite a rock.

20 April 1862

BEHOLD THE MAN

Shall Christ hang on the Cross,
    and we not look?
  Heaven, earth, and hell, stood
    gazing at the first,
  While Christ for long-cursed man
    was counted cursed;
Christ, God and Man, Whom God
    the Father strook
And shamed and sifted and one
    while forsook: –
  Cry shame upon our bodies we
    have nursed
  In sweets, our souls in pride, our
    spirits immersed
In wilfulness, our steps run all acrook.
Cry shame upon us! for He bore our
    shame
  In agony, and we look on at ease
With neither hearts on flame nor
    cheeks on flame.
  What hast thou, what have I, to
    do with peace?
Not to send peace but send a sword
    He came,
  And fire and fasts and tearful
    night watches.

Before 1882

WE PIERCED THEE

Ah Lord, we all have pierced Thee:
    wilt Thou be
  Wroth with us all to slay us all?
Nay, Lord, be this thing far from
        Thee and me:
  By whom should we arise, for we
      are small,
By whom if not by Thee?

Lord, if of us who pierced Thee
      Thou spare one,
  Spare yet one more to love Thy
      Face,
And yet another of poor souls undone,
  Another, and another – God of
      grace,
Let mercy overrun.

Before 1893

SORROW BEYOND SORROW

Lord Jesus Christ, grown faint upon
    the Cross,
  A sorrow beyond sorrow in Thy
    look,
    The unutterable craving for my
    soul;
    Thy love of me sufficed
To load upon Thee and make good
    my loss
  In face of darkened heaven and
    earth that shook: –
  In face of earth and heaven,
    take Thou my whole
    Heart, O Lord Jesus Christ.

Before 1886

THE DESCENT FROM THE CROSS

Is this the Face that thrills with awe
   Seraphs who veil their face above?
Is this the Face without a flaw,
   The Face that is the Face of Love?
Yea, this defaced, a lifeless clod,
   Hath all creation's love sufficed,
Hath satisfied the love of God,
   This Face the Face of Jesus
      Christ.

Before 1882

LIFE IS DEATH

Man's life is death. Yet Christ
 endured to live,
 Preaching and teaching, toiling
 to and fro,
Few men accepting what He yearned
 to give,
 Few men with eyes to know
 His Face, that Face of Love He
 stooped to show.

Man's death is life. For Christ
 endured to die
 In slow unuttered weariness of
 pain,
A curse and an astonishment, passed
 by,
 Pointed at, mocked again
 By men for whom He shed His
 Blood – in vain?

Before 1886

Easter

There is nothing more that they
    can do
  For all their rage and boast:
Caiaphas with his blaspheming
    crew,
  Herod with his host;

Pontius Pilate in his judgment hall
  Judging their Judge and his,
Or he who led them all and passed
    them all,
  Arch-Judas with his kiss.

The sepulchre made sure with
    ponderous stone,
  Seal that same stone, O priest:
It may be thou shalt block the
    Holy One
  From rising in the east.

Set a watch about the sepulchre
  To watch on pain of death:
They must hold fast the stone if
   One should stir
  And shake it from beneath.

God Almighty, He can break a seal,
  And roll away a stone:
Can grind the proud in dust who
    would not kneel,
  And crush the mighty one.

There is nothing more that they
    can do
  For all their passionate care,
Those who sit in dust, the blessed
    few,
  And weep and rend their hair.

Peter, Thomas, Mary Magdalen,
  The Virgin unreproved,
Joseph and Nicodemus foremost
    men,
  And John the well–beloved.

Bring your finest linen and your
    spice,
  Swathe the sacred Dead,
Bind with careful hands and piteous
    eyes
  The napkin round His head:

Lay Him in the garden-rock to rest:
  Rest you the Sabbath length:
The Sun that went down crimson in
    the west
  Shall rise renewed in strength.

God Almighty shall give joy for
    pain,
  Shall comfort him who grieves:
Lo He with joy shall doubtless come
    again
  And with Him bring His sheaves.

23 March 1861

SPRING BURSTS TODAY

Spring bursts today,
For Christ is risen and all the earth's
at play.

Flash forth, thou Sun,
The rain is over and gone, its work
is done.

Winter is past,
Sweet Spring is come at last, is come
at last.

Bud, Fig and Vine,
Bud, Olive, fat with fruit and oil and
wine.

Break forth this morn
In roses, thou but yesterday a thorn.

Uplift thy head,
O pure white Lily through the
Winter dead.

Beside your dams
Leap and rejoice, you merry-making
Lambs.

All Herds and Flocks
Rejoice, all Beasts of thickets and
of rocks.

Sing, Creatures, sing,
Angels and Men and Birds and
everything.

All notes of Doves
Fill all our world: this is the time
of loves._

Before 1882

HIS RETURNING

Words cannot utter
   Christ His returning:
Mankind, keep jubilee,
   Strip off your mourning,
Crown you with garlands,
   Set your lamps burning.

Speech is left speechless;
   Set you to singing,
Fling your hearts open wide,
   Set your bells ringing:
Christ the Chief Reaper
   Comes, His sheaf bringing.

Earth wakes her song-birds,
   Puts on her flowers,
Leads out her lambkins,
   Builds up her bowers:
This is man's spousal day,
   Christ's day and ours.

Before 1886

WORLD GROWING GREEN

Out in the rain a world is growing
    green,
  On half the trees quick buds are
     seen
    Where glued-up buds have
     been.
Out in the rain God's Acre stretches
    green,
  Its harvest quick tho' still unseen:
    For there the Life hath been.

If Christ hath died His brethren
     well may die,
  Sing in the gate of death, lay by
    This life without a sigh:
For Christ hath died and good it is
    to die;
  To sleep when so He lays us by,
    Then wake without a sigh.

Yea, Christ hath died, yea, Christ is
     risen again:
  Wherefore both life and death
     grow plain
    To us who wax and wane;
For Christ Who rose shall die no
    more again:
  Amen: till He makes all things
     plain
    Let us wax on and wane.

Before 1886

A BETTER RESURRECTION

I have no wit, no words, no tears;
  My heart within me like a stone
Is numbed too much for hopes or
    fears.
  Look right, look left, I dwell alone;
I lift mine eyes, but dimmed with
    grief
  No everlasting hills I see;
My life is in the falling leaf:
    O Jesus, quicken me.

My life is like a faded leaf,
  My harvest dwindled to a husk:
Truly my life is void and brief
  And tedious in the barren dusk;
My life is like a frozen thing,
  No bud nor greenness can I see;
Yet rise it shall – the sap of Spring;
    O Jesus, rise in me.

My life is like a broken bowl,
  A broken bowl that cannot hold
One drop of water for my soul
  Or cordial in the searching cold;
Passing away, saith my God, passing
    away:
Winter passeth after the long delay:
New grapes on the vine, new figs
    on the tender spray,
Turtle calleth turtle in Heaven's
    May.
Though I tarry, wait for Me, trust
    Me, watch and pray:

Arise, come away, night is past and
      lo it is day,
My love, My sister, My spouse, thou
      shalt hear Me say.
Then I answered: Yea.

1860

Ascension

WE PURSUE THY STEPS

O Lord Almighty Who hast formed
    us weak,
  With us whom Thou hast formed
    deal fatherly;
Be found of us whom Thou hast
    deigned to seek,
  Be found that we the more may
    seek for Thee;
Lord, speak and grant us ears to
    hear Thee speak;
  Lord, come to us and grant us
    eyes to see;
Lord, make us meek, for Thou
    Thyself art meek;
  Lord, Thou art Love, fill us with
    charity.
O Thou the Life of living and of
    dead,
  Who givest more the more
    Thyself hast given,
    Suffice us as Thy saints Thou
    hast sufficed;
That beautified, replenished,
    comforted,

Still gazing off from earth and up
at heaven,
We may pursue Thy steps,
Lord Jesus Christ.

Before 1893

A CLOUD RECEIVED HIM

When Christ went up to Heaven
    the Apostles stayed
  Gazing at Heaven with souls and
    wills on fire,
Their hearts on flight along the
    track He made,
  Winged by desire.

Their silence spake: 'Lord, why
    not follow Thee?
  Home is not home without Thy
    Blessed Face,
Life is not life. Remember, Lord,
    and see,
  Look back, embrace.

'Earth is one desert waste of
    banishment,
  Life is one long-drawn anguish of
    decay.
Where Thou wert wont to go we
    also went:
  Why not today?'

Nevertheless a cloud cut off their
    gaze:
  They tarry to build up Jerusalem,
Watching for Him, while thro' the
    appointed days
  He watches them.

They do His Will, and doing it
    rejoice,
  Patiently glad to spend and to be
    spent:
Still He speaks to them, still they
    hear His Voice
    And are content.

Whitsun

THE WHITE DOVE

The white dove cooeth in her downy
    nest,
Keeping her young ones warm
    beneath her breast:
The white moon saileth through the
    cool clear sky,
Screened by a tender mist in passing
    by:
The white rose buds, with thorns
    upon its stem,
All the more precious and more dear
    for them:
The stream shines silver in the tufted
    grass,
The white clouds scarcely dim it as
    they pass;
Deep in the valleys lily cups are
    white,
They send up incense all the holy
    night.
Our souls are white, made clean in
    Blood once shed:
White blessed Angels watch around
    our bed: —

O spotless Lamb of God, still keep
    us so,
Thou who wert born for us in time
    of snow.

1853

RUSHING WIND

At sound as of rushing wind, and
    sight as of fire,
  Lo flesh and blood made spirit
    and fiery flame,
Ambassadors in Christ's and the
    Father's Name,
  To woo back a world's desire.

These men chose death for their life
    and shame for their boast,
  For fear courage, for doubt
    intuition of faith,
  Chose love that is strong as death
    and stronger than death
  In the power of the Holy Ghost.

Before 1886

OUR WISDOM AND OUR REST

Lord Jesus Christ, our Wisdom and
   our Rest,
  Who wisely dost reveal and wisely
   hide,
  Grant us such grace in wisdom to
   abide
According to Thy Will whose Will
   is best.
Contented with Thine uttermost
   behest,
  Too sweet for envy and too high
   for pride;
  All simple-souled, dove-hearted
   and dove-eyed,
Soft-voiced, and satisfied in humble
   nest.
Wondering at the bounty of Thy
   Love
  Which gives us wings of silver
   and of gold;
  Wings folded close, yet ready to
   unfold
  When Thou shalt say, 'Winter
   is past and gone:'
When Thou shalt say, 'Spouse,
   sister, love and dove,
  Come hither, sit with Me upon
   My Throne.'

Before 1886

THE TRINITY

My God, Thyself being Love Thy
    heart is love,
  And love Thy Will and love Thy
    Word to us,
  Whether Thou show us depths
    calamitous
Or heights and flights of rapturous
    peace above.
O Christ the Lamb, O Holy Ghost
    the Dove,
  Reveal the Almighty Father unto
    us;
  That we may tread Thy courts
    felicitous,
Loving Who loves us, for our God
    is Love.
Lo, if our God be Love thro' heaven's
    long day,
  Love is He thro' our mortal
    pilgrimage,
   Love was He thro' all aeons
    that are told.
  We change, but Thou remainest;
    for Thine age
   Is, Was, and Is to come, nor
    new nor old;
We change, but Thou remainest
    yea and yea!

Before 1893

All Saints

AWAKE WITH THE SAINTS

Up, my drowsing eyes!
  Up, my sinking heart!
Up to Jesus Christ arise!
  Claim your part
In all raptures of the skies.

Yet a little while,
  Yet a little way,
Saints shall reap and rest and smile
  All the day.
Up! let's trudge another mile.

Before 1886

A MARTYR

It is over the horrible pain,
   All is over the struggle and doubt:
She's asleep though her friends stand
     and weep,
   She's asleep while the multitudes
     shout:
Not to wake to her anguish again,
   Not to wake until death is cast out.

Stoop, look at the beautiful face,
   See the smile on the satisfied
     mouth,
The hands crost – she hath
     conquered not lost:
   She hath drunk who was fevered
     with drouth:
She shall sleep in her safe resting-
     place
   While the hawk spreads her wings
     toward the South.

She shall sleep while slow seasons
     are given,
   While daylight and darkness go
     round:
Her heart is at rest in its nest,
   Her body at rest in the ground:
She has travelled the long road to
     heaven,
   She sought it and now she has
     found.

Will you follow the track that she
    trod,
  Will you tread in her footsteps,
    my friend?
That pathway is rough, but enough
  Are the light and the balm that
    attend.
Do I tread in her steps, O my God, –
  Shall I joy with her joy in the end?

23 April 1856

FOR THE LEAST OF ALL SAINTS

Love is the key of life and death,
  Of hidden heavenly mystery:
Of all Christ is, of all He saith,
    Love is the key.

As three times to His Saint He saith,
  He saith to me, He saith to thee,
Breathing His Grace-conferring
    Breath:
    'Lovest thou Me?'

Ah, Lord, I have such feeble faith,
  Such feeble hope to comfort me:
But love it is, is strong as death,
    And I love Thee.

Before 1893

AS GRAINS OF SAND

As grains of sand, as stars, as drops
    of dew,
  Numbered and treasured by the
      Almighty Hand,
  The Saints triumphant throng
      that holy land
Where all things and Jerusalem are
    new.
We know not half they sing or half
    they do,
  But this we know, they rest and
      understand;
  While like a conflagration freshly
      fanned
Their love glows upward, outward,
    thro' and thro'.
Lo like a stream of incense
      launched on flame
  Fresh Saints stream up from
      death to life above,
    To shine among those others
      and rejoice:
What matters tribulation whence
      they came?
    All love and only love can find
      a voice
  Where God makes glad His
      Saints, for God is Love.

Before 1886

Index of Titles

Index of First Lines